THE
NEIGHBORHOOD'S
CHILD

THE
NEIGHBORHOOD'S
CHILD

Peggy Seeney Caranda

ARPress
ILLUMINATING IDEAS
EMPOWERING VOICES

ARPress
45 Dan Road Suite 5
Canton MA 02021

Hotline: 1(888) 8210229
Fax: 1(508) 545-7580

Ordering Information:
Quantity sales. Special discounts are available on quantity purchases by corporations,associations, and others. For details, contact the publisher at the address above.

Printed in the United States of America.

ISBN-13:   Paperback   979-8-89356-723-6
              eBook   979-8-89356-724-3
              Hardback   979-8-89356-729-8

Library of Congress Control Number: 2024905309

THE NEIGHBORHOOD'S CHILD

Book Bags & Buster Brown Shoes

Poems & Verse from my childhood

Peggy Seeney Caranda

STORY TIME

"Miss Gertie's Girl", Peggy Seeney Caranda is
an artist, illustrator and author living in Owings
Mills, Maryland. Peggy was recognized for her
art by Zeta Phi Beta Sorority, Alpha Zeta Chapter,
as Woman of the Year in the Arts 2000.

THE NEIGHBORHOOD'S CHILD is a book
of poems and verse from Peggy's childhood
memories growing up in The Historic Upton
Community of Baltimore.

MISS GERTIE'S GIRL

Sure, is nice being Miss Gertie's Girl
Streetcar rides
Rolling down the hill in Druid Hill Park
Long walks and Lexington Market

Peanut shells and bakery smells
Sure, is nice being Miss Gertie's Girl

Howdy Doody, Dick Tracy, baby dolls
Picnic baskets and fried chicken
Sure is nice being Miss Gertie's Girl

Kisses, hugs, Sunday afternoons
Sure is nice being Miss Gertie's Girl

LITTLE CHILD YOU ARE LOVED

Mama's love
Daddy's Love
Little child you are loved

Brother's love
Sister's love
Little child you are loved

Grandma's love
Grandpa's love
Little child you are loved!

THREE ON A SCOOTER

Push, Push

Pull, Pull

Slide, Ride

Three on a scooter

Bump, Bump

Three on a scooter

Giggles, Wiggles

Tickles, Squiggles

Three on a scooter

JUST LIKE ME

I've got a sister just like me.
When she smiles
She looks just like me.

Buttons and bows
Lollipops and gum
All these things she has
Just like me

I've got a friend.
Just like me
When she cries
She feels just like me.

I've got a pal.
Just like me
When she's happy

She laughs just like me.
That's my sister.
Just like me

MR. CHICKEN MAN

Oh what a bright and beautiful day
Dad is out and on his way
Selling eggs and chickens making his pay

The lady down the street yells
Hey! Mr. Chicken Man
Come this way

It's been a good and fruitful day
All the chickens and all the eggs
Been sold by now

Dad tips his hat and says
Much obliged, much obliged

It's been a mighty fine day

AIN'T SHE CUTE

Little girl in yellow

She sure is cute

Black patent shoes

White anklet socks

She sure is cute

Mama's waiting

Daddy's pacing

Little girl in yellow

She sure is cute

ORCHARD STREET

It's the church down the street

Orchard Street

It's the church with the big pews

Orchard Street

It's the church with the stained glass windows

Orchard Street

It's the church where angels sing

Orchard Street

NIGHT OF THE CHILLER

Up I sprang.
When the doorbell rang
It was the night of ghosts and goblins.

Slowly I edged to peer through the door.
When up I sprang
As the doorbell rang

To my surprise
There stood a sight.
It was a night of chills and thrills.

With trembling knees, I backed away.
But up I sprang.
When the doorbell rang

Someone called out.
Sister, sister opens the door.
It's only us who come to bring you cheer.

So up I sprang.
When the doorbell rang

WENDY AND ME

Pigtails and ribbons

Book bags and Buster Brown shoes

Baby Ruths, and bubble gum

Wendy and me

Sugar and Spice

Everything's nice.

With Wendy and Me

STEP SITTERS

Playing jacks
Singing songs of verse
Hand jive, ham bone

My cousins and I were the step sitters
Playing games and singing songs
We better not leave those steps

When six o'clock came around
You could find us sitting on the steps
Playing games and singing songs

Find the stone in your hand
Singing ham bone where you been
We better not leave those steps

When nine o'clock came around
We were in the house fast asleep.

The Step Sitters

MISS QUEENIE AND FEATHER

Downstairs their lives
A lady and her son
Miss Queenie and Feather

Pots of cabbage
Pans of ham
On the stove smelling good

Miss Queenie and Feather
Invite us to come to sit a spell.
And have a bite to eat.

My cousin and I
All aglow with eager anticipation
Cause Miss Queenie and Feather
Invite us to dinner.
So, at the table we sit

Napkins under our chins
Forks in hand
We eat our meal.
It's so nice.

Miss Queenie and Feather
Invited us to come and sit a spell.

GRANDMA'S SWITCH

It was a sunny afternoon.
When Grandma set me straight
She let me know she will not tolerate
Any misbehavior

So off I went to play.
A game of hide and seek.
Knowing that out in front I was to stay.

So, if I was to stray.
Grandma's switch
I would get straight away.

But as children often do
Away I went down the street to play.
When in the distance I heard Grandma say

It is time to come in and stay.
For since I went astray
Grandma's switch I would get right away.

DO YOU KNOW TWEEDY AND DUTT

Do you know Tweedy and Dutt?
Yes, I know the little girl.
Down the street with the squiggly hair
And her brother Dutt

Sometimes when we are out and about.
Eating ice cream and drinking soda pop

I smile and say to myself.
What good friends we are
Yes, I know Tweedy and Dutt

THE TOOTH FAIRY

Oh, what a bright and beautiful morning
As I sit in my chair
Eating crunchy little round oats

When suddenly something hard I bite
I reach into my mouth from which I pull my tooth.
It is a wonder, but mama says it will grow back.

If I am good and place it under my pillow tonight
The Tooth Fairy will come.
And leave me delight.

MY DADDY'S GARDEN

Daffodils and gladiolas

Planting flowers in my daddy's garden

Pinwheels and swans

Bright sunny days and roses

Little hands and sun hats

Playfully sifting and digging

While planting flowers in my daddy's garden

THE MAGIC READING ROOM

When I want to travel the worldwide
I just visited the room where angels sing.
And knights in shinning armor shine

Where children, black, yellow, brown and white
Play games and dance.
Where castles of old and men are bold
It's called The Magic Reading Room

When I want to pretend, I'm dressed in gold.
Or in gossamer folds

I just open a book from
The Magic Reading Room
The world is bright.
Stars shine at night.
Blue skies turn purple with light.

So, let us gather our things
And spread our wings.
As we travel together
In The Magic Reading Room

FRIED EGGS, BISCUITS AND BACON

The morning lights.
Begins to creep.
Through my eyes

I turn my face to the pillow.
Trying not to awake
Pots and pans clanging.

Coffee smells
Fried eggs, biscuits and bacon
Oh, what a day this is going to be

I rub the sleep from my eyes.
And sit on the side of the bed.
My feet hit the cold floor.

But I don't mind.
Because fried eggs, biscuits and bacon are
waiting.

PICK UP STICKS

One, two pick up sticks.

Three, four, shut the door.

Red, green, blue and yellow

Five, six, seven, eight

Flip, flop, move a color.

It's a fun game we play.

When we try

To pick up sticks

ICKY STICKY COTTON CANDY

Mr. Bill told Missy, Mike and Duke that he was going to take them to the Candy Land Amusement Park on the weekend. Mike and Duke asked their parents for permission to go. Mr. Bill was Missy's father.

By Saturday morning, everyone was dressed and ready to go. They all piled into Mr. Bill's car, and off they headed to the amusement park.

Along the way they saw a Merry Dairy Ice Cream store. They stopped to get a soft frozen vanilla cone.

As soon as they arrived at the Candy Land Amusement Park, they all ran to the Fun House. The first room had squiggly mirrors that made everyone look funny.

The next room had scary hands reaching out to grab them as they walked by. Then they crawled through a rolling barrel. Oh, they were having so much fun.

Missy, Duke and Mike wanted to get on the Flash Dash Roller Coaster. From a distance it looked like it would be fun.

Mr. Bill and the children got on the roller coaster. Up in the air it went high in the sky. Then suddenly The Flash Dash Roller Coaster dropped down and swung low to the ground. They all screamed with delight. Soon they were dizzy and tired.

As they stumbled off the roller coaster, they walked to the Icky Sticky Cotton Candy stand. There they each got pink cotton candy on a stick. It was such a fun day.

Falling asleep in the car on the way home, Missy, Duke and Mike smiled and dreamed of icky, sticky cotton candy at the Candy Land Amusement Park.

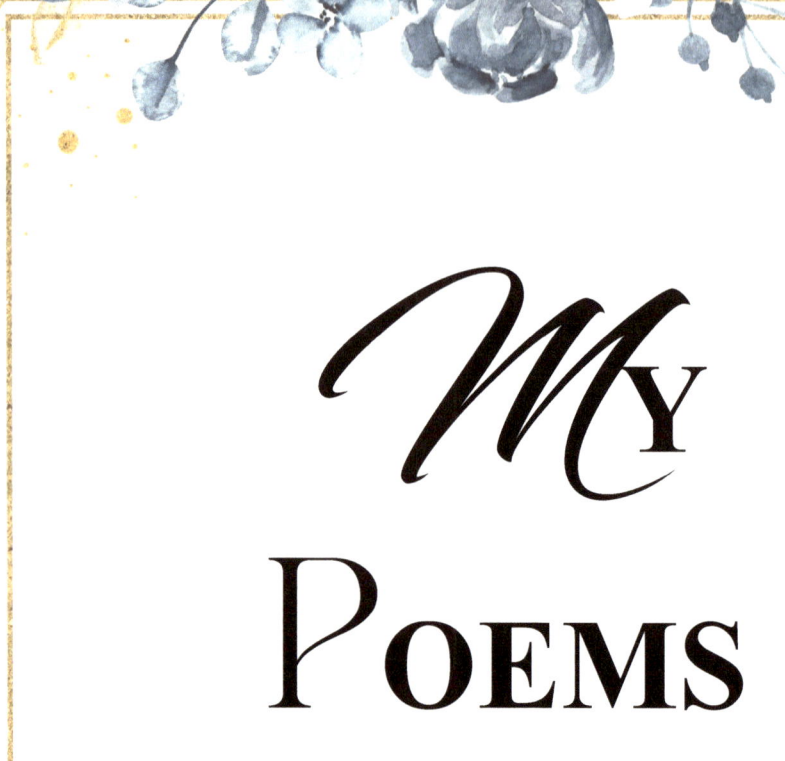

My
Poems

BIRTHDAY PARTY

Pin the tail on the donkey.
Balloons, hats and horns
Ice cream and cake.

Five-year-olds
Boys and girls
Jumping, hopping, running

It is time.
When you must go home

Wrapping paper, boxes with ribbons
Bright colored tissue paper

It is time.
When you must go home

Blowing out the candles
Singing Happy Birthday

It is time.
When you must go home

EENY, WEENY, TEENY BEENY

Well Beeny is just a little bug.
That wanted to leave its Eeny, Weeny, Teeny bug hut
To see the world around it
So, one day Beeny set off on an Eeny, weeny trip

It was a bright and sunny day.
The grass was green.
The leaves on the trees were blowing in the warm breeze.
The flowers were bursting with vivid colors.

First Beeny saw a garden full of yellow sunflowers
with soft brown faces.
So, Beeny crawled up one stem and said
"Hello Ms Sunflower"

Ms Sunflower smiled and said.
"Why hello little Beeny
How are you this nice fine day?"

Beeny than traveled a little way down the road.
There in the bright sunshine
Beeny came upon a bed of roses.

Some roses were red.
Other roses were pink and white.
Beeny sniffed and wriggled his nose.
The smell of perfume filled the air.

Beeny crawled up one rose stem.
Careful not to step on a thorn.
He greeted a red rose.

The rose smiled and said.
"Why it's eeny, weeny, teeny Beeny
Come to say hello."

Over in the corner
There was a strange web attached to a house.
Beeny curiously crawled over to see what it was.

Suddenly a spider
Looked at Beeny and said.
"You better not tear my web."

Beeny quickly crawled away.
Getting tired, Beeny began its journey back home.
Beeny wanted to get home.

Before the sun went to bed for the night

Crawling slowly
Beeny waved goodbye to Mr. Sun
While passing the bed of roses
They waved goodbye too

As Beeny passed Ms Sunflower
She said "Good night Beeny
Hope to see you soon someday"

BALDINI MILK CUT

The squiggly hair boy down the street
His hair is cut so short
Everyone teases and call him Baldini Milk Cut
Don't know why his mother cut his hair so
short

When he goes out to put out the trash
I run to the window and yell
Hey Baldini Milk Cut

Don't know why his mother cut his hair so
short
He only smiles and waves
Because he agrees

Don't know why his mother cut his hair so
short

RED RIDER AT THE FULTON

Saturday mornings

My brothers and I

Red Rider, The Lone Ranger, The Cisco Kid

Hot dogs and soda pop

Every Saturday at the Fulton movies

My brothers and I rushing down the aisles

Just trying to get a front row seat

Ushers saying hush

You better not rush

Laughing, giggling, eating

Usher saying hush

You better rush

The movies are over

The lights are up

We better rush

Because Daddy's coming

DO NOT PASS GO

Park Place

Do not pass go

Water works

Do not pass go

Boardwalk

Do not pass go

Top Hat, Thimble

Thank you

Do Not Pass Go

JOHNNY ON THE FIRST STEP

The night was hot and sticky.
My cousin and I sat on the back porch.
In the darkness telling stories and
spinning tales

I closed my eyes and leaned back in my
chair.
Already to enjoy the dark night with

Sparkling stars in the sky

As usual we were telling stories and
spinning tales.

When cousin started to spin a new story
I opened my eyes wide to listen, with rapt
attention.
Thus began the tale of Johnny on the first
step.

Johnny was coming to get us.
Creeping quietly up the stairs
The steps began to creek as
Johnny began to ascend.
He was on the first step.
Then the second
Next the third
Then the fourth and fifth steps

As the night closed in around me
I began to shake and tremble.
Fright clutching at my throat.
Cousin was telling stories and spinning

tales.

Just as I leaned forward to listen more closely.
A hand reached out in the dark and clutched my back.

I jumped out of my chair.
Ran in the house.
Closed my bedroom door.
Sank beneath the covers.
Hoping that Johnny was on the first step.

A CHILD'S MEALTIME BLESSING

God is Great

God is Good

Let us thank him for our food.

By His hands we all are fed

Give us Lord our Daily Bread

Amen

NOW I LAY ME DOWN TO SLEEP

Thank you, Lord, for another day

The chance to learn, the chance to play.

Now as I lay me down to sleep.

I pray the Lord my soul to keep.

Please, guard me safe till morning light.

But should I die before I wake?

I pray the Lord my soul to take.

And should I live for other days?

I pray that God will guide my ways.

Amen

IN MY HEART I KNOW WHO I AM

Affirmations for Children

Every day in every way

I will be very happy.

I will be very strong.

I will be self-confident.

At home

At school

On the playground

I know that I am loved.

I am smart.

I am important and beautiful.

I know that I am talented.

I will be successful.

I am a blessed child of God.

Dream of a world.

Build a world.

If I can perceive it

I can achieve it.

GUM DROPS & LOLLIPOP SWIRLS

Tweedy, Dutt and Feather were on their way to the store to buy milk and bread for Miss Queenie. Along the way they decided to stop at the candy store in the middle of the block on Riggs Avenue.

Their eyes lit up with the sight of the jars of brightly colored gum drops, orange leaves, green leaves and large lollipop swirls on a stick. There on the counter were bags of Sugar Daddy candies, sweet onion balls, and bright red candy apples. They looked at each other with dismay, because they didn't have money to buy the sweet treats.

So off they went to complete their task. Suddenly, Dutt stated he knew how they could get the money to buy the candy. He said he would offer to put out the trash for Mrs. Pinkney down the street, since she was in need of help.

Feather stated he could run errands for Mrs. Hall, who always wanted someone to go to the store for her. Tweedy stated she could babysit for Mrs. Johnson. At the end of the week, they all had earned some money from doing work for their neighbors who were very happy for their help. Tweedy, Dutt and Feather returned to the candy store with their well-earned money. They each picked out their favorite treat.

Dutt picked a bag of gum drops. Tweedy picked the lollipop swirl on a stick. Feather decided on a sweet onion ball. Miss Queenie was so proud of them that she rewarded each of them with a hug.

MY PAL ROCKY

Rocky has lost his green ball.

And does not know where to find it.
He looks here.
He looks there.
And where oh where can it be

Leave him alone.
And soon he will find it.
Oh, there it is behind the chair

It is a bright and sunny day.
Rocky and I go for a walk and play.

He jumps and runs.
Along the way
As he greets all who pass us by
And does not go astray.

Rocky runs up the hill.
To catch his ball

He runs up and down.
And all around

Now after a long day
Of play

It is time to say.

Good night

And sleep tight.

HIPPITY HOPPITY BUNNY

Hippity Hoppity Bunny is coming.
With special gifts for each boy and girl

Hippity has jellybeans.
Chocolate eggs
Marshmallow yellow chicks
That makes you smile with joy.

Chocolate bunnies
Colored hard-boiled eggs
Filling your Easter Basket

Hippity hops up and down.
Going along his way
Bringing happiness to every smiling face

Oh, what a wonderful day
With pretty bonnets
Easter lilies and top hats

Little girls and boys
All dressed up.
Ready for a fun day

Hippity Hoppity Bunny

So happy for such a fun and happy day

LADY GINGER SPICE GIRL

Sugar and spice
Everything's nice.
With Ginger Spice

Ginger is tan and white.
Her eyes are black and bright.
She knows how to get her way.
By wriggling her tail to play

Ginger's favorite toy is a red ball.
She bats it high.
She bats it low.
And when she can
She lets it go.

When it's time to eat
She gets her bowl and treats.
So, let me say
What a loveable puppy she is today

Ginger is so funny.
Like a little bunny
So soft and cuddly
You want to hold her close.
And caress her fondly.

My Morkie
Is part Yorkie
A very nice Lady
Ginger Spice Girl

THUNDER THE PASTEL PONY

Thunder is a pretty little pony
And my best friend forever

Thunder has a flowing mane.
A fluffy tail
That swishes back and forth

Thunder likes to eat apples and carrots.
Sugar cubes are his favorite treat.

When Thunder goes out to see
What the day will bring
He nods his head to say hello.
To the birds tweeting in the trees

Thunder prances and gallops
Across the field
The wind was sweeping across his face.

One day Thunder stepped on my foot.
When I yelped

Thunder lowered his head to kiss me on my forehead.

My pastel pony
Thunder is the sweetest, best friend

COME DANCE WITH ME

Jitterbug, mash potato, hand jive.
Buddy Dean, Soul Train
The Madison, Fat Daddy, Hot Rod

Come Dance with Me

Backward slop, the jerk
Saturday nights
Blue lights, the grind

Come Dance with Me

The twist, the bump, the electric slide
Moon walk, Michael Jackson, Thriller

Come Dance with Me

Dip, whip, split.
Wobble, bobble, and hobble.
Stomp the floor.

Come Dance with Me

LAZY HAZY DAYS OF SUMMER

School is out, no more pencils and no more books.

Sitting on the porch

Swatting flies and counting cars

Hot summer days and sweaty nights

Listening for the jingle, jingle

The Good Humor Man

Bringing popsicles and cones

Oh, for those lazy days of summer

SNOWBALLS AND SNOWFLAKES

Looking out the window
Watching the snowflakes fall
The snow piles high on the steps
It's so high you can't even see the sidewalk.

Soon as it stops.
Kids on the block come out to play.
Some build snowmen
Others ride a trash can at the top down the
hill.

The kids across the street make snowballs.
Edgy tells Billy, we are going to play.
The game of snow brigade

Jill finishes her snowman.
She asks can she play too.

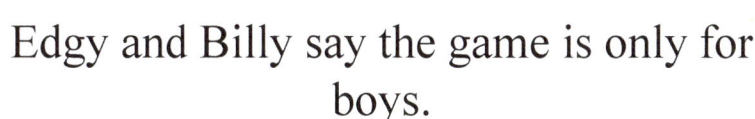

Edgy and Billy say the game is only for boys.
Girls may get hurt.
But Jill says she can play just as well as they

With snowballs flying through the air
Splat, splat.
They all fall down covered in the fluffy

snow

SANDMICHES

In my neighborhood
We ate sandwiches.
But I like sandmiches

The usual peanut butter and jelly
Tuna fish and potato chips
These are the sandwiches we eat.

But the sandmiches
Are what I like best

Some are mustard.
Others are mayonnaise.
The best is syrup on toast.
May I boast.

We sit in a corner.
Like Jack Horner
Or little Miss Muffet
We sit on our tuffet.
Eating our sandmiches away

THE SQUIGGLY KIDS

One day Tweedy, Dutt and Feather decided to venture out beyond their neighborhood. However, Miss Queenie warned them not to go to far from in front of their house. She wanted to be able to see them playing.

Off they went down the street, giggling and skipping. The three children ran down the street and around the corner. Before they knew it they had gone too far and were lost.

Tweedy, Dutt and Feather walked up one street and then another. Nothing looked familiar.

They decided to knock on a friendly-looking door. A little old lady came to the door and stated, "Oh my, what cute little children". She said, "What can I do for you today?"

"We are lost" stated Feather. "We can't find our way back home", Dutt whispered in a low voice. Tweedy cried, "I want my Mother!"

The little old lady asked if they would like a glass of milk and a cookie. They all nodded in agreement. As she began to pour each of them a glass of milk, the little old lady began to tell them a story about three little children who disobeyed their parents.

The three little children were lost. A mean old witch captured them. The witch decided to put the children in her oven and cook them for dinner.

Tweedy, Dutt and Feather began to shake and tremble as they listened to the story. They were scared that the witch would cook them for dinner.

Dutt was quiet. Tweedy began to cry. Feather pretended to be brave.

Just as they finished their milk and cookies, the little old lady asked if they knew their address. Feather quickly responded giving his address and telephone number.

The little old lady went to the oven and opened the door as she turned up the temperature. She left the oven door open and left the room. The little old lady told the children she would return soon.

The children each looked at the open oven and wondered what would happen to them for disobeying their parents.

Tweedy, Dutt and Feather sat nervously at the table. They watched as the sun went down and it began to get dark.

It seemed as if hours passed as they waited for the little old lady to return to the kitchen. The room got warmer and warmer. They huddled together shaking with anticipation.

Suddenly, to their relief Feather's mother, Miss Queenie, appeared in the doorway. They each ran to her with tears in their eyes.

Walking home in the moonlight, they each tried to tell Miss Queenie that they were afraid of what would happen to them. They each promised never to leave their neighborhood again without their parents' permission.

NEIGHBORHOOD CHILD PROMO

COME TO THE MAGIC READING ROOM WHERE KNIGHTS IN SHINING ARMOR ARE BOLD, MELVIN THE FANTASTIC BIRD FLYS AWAY TO A FOREIGN LAND AND CHILDREN TAKE A RIDE ON A ROLLER COASTER AT THE CANDY LAND AMUSEMENT PARK.

THE CAROLINE CENTER

BALTIMORE BOOK FESTIVAL